BEHIND THE CURTAIN
Act Out History

A LEVEE BROKE

HURRICANE KATRINA AND AMERICA'S RESPONSE

Virginia Loh-Hagan

T0062296

45TH PARALLEL PRESS

Published in the United States of America by Cherry Lake Publishing
Ann Arbor, Michigan
www.cherrylakepublishing.com

Reading Adviser: Beth Walker Gambro, MS, Ed., Reading Consultant, Yorkville, IL
Cover Designer: Felicia Macheske

Photo Credits: © Gary Paul Lewis/Shutterstock.com, cover, 1; © lavizzara/Shutterstock.com, 5; © Wirestock Creators/Shutterstock.com, 6; © Marin James/Shutterstock.com, 9; © Jozef Jankola/Shutterstock.com, 11; © Pattie Steib/Shutterstock.com, 12; © Chattaphan Sakult/Shutterstock.com, 15; © Brian Nolan/Shutterstock.com, 17; © TadDenson/Shutterstock.com, 19; © Wirestock Images/Shutterstock.com, 22, 25

Graphic Elements Throughout: © Chipmunk131/Shutterstock.com; © Nowik Sylwia/Shutterstock.com; © Andrey_Popov/Shutterstock.com; © NadzeyaShanchuk/Shutterstock.com; © KathyGold/Shutterstock.com; © Black creator/Shutterstock.com; © Edvard Molnar/Shutterstock.com; © Elenadesign/Shutterstock.com; © estherpoon/Shutterstock.com

45th Parallel Press is an imprint of Cherry Lake Publishing.

Library of Congress Cataloging-in-Publication Data
Names: Loh-Hagan, Virginia, author.
Title: A levee broke : Hurricane Katrina and America's response / by Virginia Loh-Hagan.
Description: Ann Arbor, Michigan : Cherry Lake Publishing, 2022. | Series: Behind the curtain
Identifiers: LCCN 2021037474 | ISBN 9781534199484 (hardcover) | ISBN 9781668900628 (paperback) |
    ISBN 9781668906385 (ebook) | ISBN 9781668902066 (pdf)
Subjects: LCSH: Hurricane Katrina, 2005—Juvenile literature. | Emergency management—Louisiana—New Orleans—
    Juvenile literature.
Classification: LCC HV636 2005 .N4 L48 2022 | DDC 363.34/92209763—dc23
LC record available at https://lccn.loc.gov/2021037474

Cherry Lake Publishing would like to acknowledge the work of the Partnership for 21st Century Learning,
a Network of Battelle for Kids. Please visit *http://www.battelleforkids.org/networks/p21* for more information.

Printed in the United States of America
Corporate Graphics

A Note on Dramatic Retellings

Participating in Readers Theater, or dramatic retellings, can greatly improve reading skills, especially fluency. The books in the **BEHIND THE CURTAIN** series give readers opportunities to learn about important historical events in a fun and engaging way. These books serve as a bridge to more complex texts. All the characters and stories have been fictionalized. To learn more, check out the Perspectives Library series and the Modern Perspectives series, as **BEHIND THE CURTAIN** books are aligned to these stories.

TABLE of CONTENTS

HISTORICAL BACKGROUND

Hurricane Katrina is one of the worst storms in U.S. history. It hit New Orleans, Louisiana, on August 29, 2005. More than 1,800 people died. The storm caused more than $100 billion in damages.

City leaders ordered an evacuation of the city. Tens of thousands of people fled. But many couldn't leave. Poor and elderly people stayed. People who lacked transportation stayed. Some sheltered in their homes. Some sheltered at the Superdome.

The Superdome is the city's sports arena. It's on higher ground. It was a "shelter of last resort." Between 20,000 to 30,000 people stayed at the Superdome. They struggled to find food and supplies.

FLASH FACT!

Hurricane Katrina displaced more than 1 million people. New Orleans is a different city today.

Vocabulary

hurricane (HUHR-uh-kayn) a severe tropical storm with high winds and heavy rains

evacuation (ih-va-kyoo-AY-shuhn) the act of moving people from a dangerous place

sheltered (SHEL-tuhrd) found protection from danger

last resort (LAST rih-ZORT) a final course of action used when all else failed

5

FLASH FACT!

Many countries helped
Katrina survivors.
Kuwait donated the most.
It donated $500 million.

Vocabulary

levees (LEH-veez) walls that
stop waterways from overflowing
and flooding nearby areas

stranded (STRAN-duhd)
being left behind

Coast Guard (KOHST GARHD)
a branch of the U.S. armed forces
responsible for the protection of
life and property at sea

Katrina's winds were strong. They wrecked buildings. They wrecked trees. The greatest damage was caused when levees broke. Storm water flooded the city. Heavy rains flooded the city. About 80 percent of the city was underwater.

The storm passed. But the city was in ruins. Buildings collapsed. People and animals were stranded. There was no water or food.

Many people helped. The Coast Guard rescued people. People moved around in boats. They offered food. People from all over sent supplies and money.

President George W. Bush didn't realize how bad things were. The government's response upset people. It failed to act quickly enough. It didn't have a strong emergency plan.

CAST of CHARACTERS

NARRATOR: person who helps tells the story

SUSAN: a young survivor of Hurricane Katrina; Philip's younger sister

PHILIP: a young survivor of Hurricane Katrina; Susan's older brother

SAM: a rescue worker with the Coast Guard

REBECCA: a survivor of Hurricane Katrina; the mother of Philip and Susan

SPOTLIGHT
AMPLIFICATION OF AN ACTIVIST

Colette Pichon Battle is a climate justice activist. She's a lawyer. Her family lost everything in Hurricane Katrina. She helps Black communities that are still recovering from Katrina. She provides free legal help and education programs. She teaches people about climate impacts. She's worried about rising sea levels. She's worried about stronger storms. Climate change threatens to erase her community. Battle said, ". . . more than 180 million people will be displaced due to climate change . . . south Louisiana is losing land at one of the fastest rates on the planet. We must start preparing for global migration today." Migration is when people move from one place to another. Not everyone can move easily. Battle worries people of color will be left behind. She wants more resources to serve her communities.

FLASH FACT!

President Barack Obama said, "What started out as a natural disaster became a man-made disaster— a failure of government to look out for its own citizens."

ACT 1

NARRATOR: *It's September 1, 2005. Hurricane Katrina hit 3 days before.* **SUSAN** *and* **PHILIP** *are in New Orleans. Their neighborhood is flooded. They're in their* **attic***.*

SUSAN: It's so hot in here!

PHILIP: It has to be more than 100 degrees Fahrenheit (38 degrees Celsius).

SUSAN: Why can't we go downstairs?

PHILIP: The house is flooded. Water is everywhere. It's not safe to go down there.

SUSAN: I'm not afraid of water. I love the pool.

PHILIP: Floodwater is not like pool water.

SUSAN: I'm a good swimmer. We can swim to safety.

PHILIP: Trust me. You don't want to swim in the floodwater. Floodwater is dangerous. It has a lot of broken bits. It has sharp objects. People can get cut. Floodwater is also **toxic**. It has waste and germs. People can get really sick. They can also drown.

Vocabulary

attic (A-tik) a space or room just below the roof of a building

toxic (TAAK-suhk) poisonous

FLASH FACT!

Drowning is the leading cause of death in floods.

SUSAN: Where did the water come from?

PHILIP: Our city is shaped like a bowl. We're below sea level. Our neighborhood is even lower than other areas.

SUSAN: Why is that?

PHILIP: Our houses are less expensive than the ones on higher ground. When it floods, we get more floodwater.

SUSAN: But how did the water get here in the first place?

PHILIP: We're surrounded by water.

SUSAN: I know about this! I learned about this in school. Lake Pontchartrain is north of us. The Mississippi River is south of us. **Swamps** are on the east and west.

PHILIP: That's correct. To protect us from floods, we have levees. But Katrina was too strong. It broke the levees.

SUSAN: I see what happened. Water came flooding in.

PHILIP: Since we're in a bowl, water is trapped here.

Vocabulary
swamps (SWAHMPS) areas of wet, spongy lands

FLASH FACT!
The houses in the higher areas recovered more quickly. They had the least amount of damage.

SUSAN: Why can't we just pump it out? Isn't that what we do during heavy rain seasons?

PHILIP: Katrina broke many of the pump stations. The president has to help us.

SUSAN: We've been stuck here for 3 days already. I'm worried about Buddy. We need to go find him.

PHILIP: Dogs are really smart. Let's hope Buddy finds his way home.

SUSAN: When are Mom and Dad coming back? I'm hungry. I'm thirsty.

PHILIP: Soon. They took our little boat. They went to find food and water.

SUSAN: They're rowing boats on top of our houses.

SPOTLIGHT
A SPECIAL EFFECT

Hurricanes have been happening forever. But scientists have been studying them for only the past 100 years. Hurricanes are huge. Scientists need modern technology to study them. They name them so they can track them. Until the 1950s, storm names were numbers. This got confusing. Words are easier to remember. The World Meteorological Organization created a system to name storms. These names are in alphabetical order. There's a list of male and female names. These names are reused every 6 years. For deadly storms, the names are retired. This means the names aren't used again. Katrina is an example. It was a deadly, costly storm. That's why it won't be used to describe another storm. This honors the people who died. It also allows us to refer to it.

FLASH FACT!

About 250,000 dogs and cats were lost or died. Disaster plans need to include ways to help animals.

PHILIP: Some people are floating around on their mattresses.

SUSAN: That's so weird.

PHILIP: Everything is weird right now. Who knew we'd be living in our attic?

SUSAN: I don't want to be here anymore. It smells really bad. I want to use a real toilet. I want to eat real food. I want to sleep in a real bed.

PHILIP: This is hard. Hopefully, Mom and Dad found help.

SUSAN: Why didn't we leave the city? Aunt Barb left.

PHILIP: Not everyone can leave. We don't know anyone outside of the city. We don't have money for a hotel. We don't have a car.

SUSAN: We could have gone with Aunt Barb.

PHILIP: Aunt Barb didn't have room for all of us. Mom and Dad wanted us to stay together.

SUSAN: Plus, we can't leave Grandpa and Grandma. I hope they're okay.

PHILIP: They're at the **nursing home**. I'm sure people are taking care of them.

Vocabulary
nursing home (NUHR-sing HOHM)
a place that takes care of elderly people

FLASH FACT!
Some people were given one-way flight tickets. They didn't have enough money to fly back home.

SUSAN: There are so many people who need help.

PHILIP: We didn't think things were going to be this bad. Hurricanes have hit our city before. We've been fine.

SUSAN: Katrina is one of the worst hurricanes ever. That's what the TV said.

PHILIP: We are here now. We will get through this.

SUSAN: Did you hear that? Look out the window. What do you see?

PHILIP: It's a helicopter. Rescue workers are at our neighbors' house.

SUSAN: What are they doing?

PHILIP: They're pulling people onto the roofs. They're putting them into the helicopter. They're here to save us!

SUSAN: But what about Mom and Dad?

PHILIP: They told me to go if rescue workers came. They said they'll find us.

SUSAN: Wave your hand out the window. Yell at them. Let them know we're here!

FLASH FACT!

Scientists say hurricanes hit the New Orleans area once every 2.8 years.

NARRATOR: SAM *is a rescue worker. He is in the helicopter. He sees* **SUSAN** *and* **PHILIP.**

SAM: Hello! I'm from the Coast Guard. I'm going to help you out of here.

SUSAN: Thank you!

SAM: Stand back. We have to use this axe. We have to break through your roof.

PHILIP: We'll get out of the way.

NARRATOR: *Sam rescues Susan and Philip. They're in the helicopter. They're with other survivors.*

PHILIP: Thanks for coming to get us.

SAM: Your parents told us you were here. We came as soon as we could.

SUSAN: You've seen my mom and dad?

SAM: Yes, they're at the Superdome. That's where we're taking you now. A lot of people are already there.

PHILIP: I see a **convoy** of trucks. They're heading to the Superdome. What are they doing?

Vocabulary
convoy (KAHN-voy) a group of ships or cars traveling together

FLASH FACT!

Each year, the Coast Guard saves about 4,000 lives. They serve in more than 20,000 search and rescue cases.

SAM: That's the **National Guard**. They're bringing food, water, and supplies.

SUSAN: That's great. We need those things.

Vocabulary
National Guard (NA-shuh-nuhl GARHD) civilians who are called to military service in emergencies

FLASH FACT!

More than 50,000 National Guard members helped with Hurricane Katrina.

SAM: Unfortunately, it's not enough. We need a lot more. We've rescued more people than there are supplies. There are still more people who need to be rescued.

PHILIP: I see people on their rooftops. They're shouting for help.

SAM: We have to come back and get them. There's not enough room in the helicopter.

PHILIP: Have you been doing this work for a long time?

SAM: I've rescued people from mountainsides. I've rescued people from tall trees. I've rescued people from ships. This is the first time I've rescued people from housetops.

SUSAN: That must be hard work.

SAM: It's easier than rescuing people on the streets. We have to avoid hitting things.

NARRATOR: *They land at the Superdome. Susan and Philip are **reunited** with their mom,* **REBECCA***.*

SUSAN: Where's Dad?

REBECCA: There aren't enough rescue workers. Your dad offered to help. He took out our boat. He's searching for people. He's bringing them back here.

SUSAN: Our boat holds only 2 people.

REBECCA: That's why it's taking him so long. He brings back 1 person at a time.

Vocabulary
reunited (ree-yoo-NYE-tuhd)
brought together again

FLASH FACT!
Katrina was the third time the Superdome was used as a storm shelter.

SUSAN: What about Grandpa and Grandma?

REBECCA: They're being evacuated. Nursing homes are putting them on buses. Buses are bringing them here. We'll be reunited with them soon.

PHILIP: There are so many people here. It's crowded.

SUSAN: It smells worse than our attic. It's also hotter.

PHILIP: This is a sports arena. It has air-conditioning. Why isn't it on?

REBECCA: It's broken. Katrina has cut off power sources.

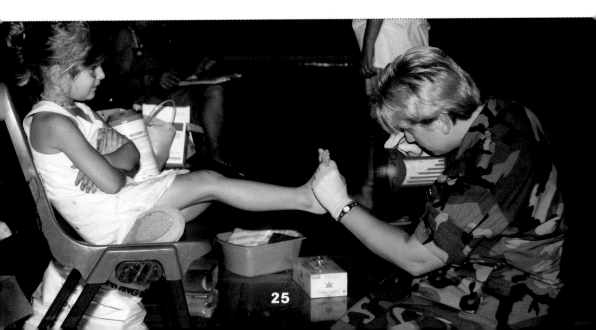

PHILIP: What happened over there?

REBECCA: The wind tore off part of the roof. Water poured onto the field.

NARRATOR: *A police officer walks by with a shouting man.*

SUSAN: Where's the police officer taking that man?

REBECCA: They made a jail cell in the basement. People are **desperate**. Some people have been **looting**. Some people are hurting others.

SUSAN: Mom, I'm hungry. Can we get some food?

REBECCA: We have to wait for new supplies to come. They're **rationing** the food. We get only so much food each day. We get 2 bottles of water. We get 2 boxed meals.

PHILIP: I have to go to the bathroom.

SPOTLIGHT
EXTRA! EXTRA! BONUS FACT!

Hurricane Katrina impacted people in different ways. Poor people suffered more. People of color suffered more. One of the biggest issues was food shortages. Stores weren't open for weeks. Lands were swamped. New Orleans became a food desert. Many people had little or no access to food. After Katrina, community gardens increased. Katherine Egland wanted to help. She asked churches to use their land to grow fruit trees. This way, churches could trade fruit. The New Orleans Food and Farm Network (NOFFN) supports urban farming. Katrina tripled the number of empty lots. NOFFN helps people transform these spaces. They turn empty lots into urban farms. Little Sparrow is the name of one of these farms. It used to be a drug corner. Today, it provides herbs and vegetables to neighbors and a nearby restaurant.

Vocabulary
desperate (DEH-spuh-ruht) hopeless

looting (LOO-ting) stealing

rationing (RA-shuh-ning) providing fixed amounts

FLASH FACT!
Local, state, and federal officials failed to help people of color. Slow actions resulted in more hardships and deaths.

REBECCA: The toilets are broken. They're overflowing. People are peeing on the floors instead.

SUSAN: Why are we here? This place sounds horrible.

REBECCA: I know this is hard to believe. But we're safer here. We're on higher ground. There's water all around us.

PHILIP: Maybe we should go back home?

REBECCA: We don't have a home anymore. We've lost everything. It'll be too hard to rebuild.

SUSAN: What are we going to do?

REBECCA: We're going to take this one step at a time.

PHILIP: And we'll do it together.

REBECCA: Things are bad. But people are helping. **Volunteers** are trying to make things better.

SUSAN: I see a lot of school buses. But people are getting on. They're not getting off.

REBECCA: They're sending people to other places for safety.

PHILIP: Where are they sending people?

REBECCA: Some are going to other cities in Louisiana. Some are going to Houston. We just have to wait and see what happens to us.

Vocabulary
volunteers (vah-luhn-TEERZ) people who donate their time or money for a cause

FLASH FACT!
Officials spent a lot of money on restoring order in the Superdome. This left fewer resources for other work that needed to be done.

FLASH FORWARD
CURRENT CONNECTIONS

Hurricane Katrina happened in 2005. But its legacy lives on. We are still feeling its effects. There is still so much work for us to do.

- **Stop global warming:** Some experts say Katrina was made worse because of global warming. Global warming is the long-term heating of Earth's climate. As ocean water heats up, hot water vapor releases into the air. Hurricanes pick up this water. The hot water acts like fuel. Hurricanes grow in power as they head toward land. They move more slowly. They can cause more damage. It's important to take care of our planet.

- **Fight against environmental racism:** Hurricane Katrina exposed how unfairly Black communities have been treated. Racism has affected many Black communities. In New Orleans, people of color are more likely to live in lower land levels. This means they got the worst flooding. During the recovery, Black communities were the last to get assistance. Their neighborhoods were redeveloped last. It is important for us to honor the basic needs of all people.

- **Be ready for emergencies:** New Orleans relies on levees and floodwalls. Before Katrina, scientists worried about the levees. They didn't think the levees were strong enough. The city's levees were designed for Category 3 storms. Katrina was a Category 5 storm. Cities need to protect themselves. They need to spend money. They need to stay updated. It's important to always be prepared.

CONSIDER THIS!

TAKE A POSITION! George W. Bush was president during Hurricane Katrina. Many people question his leadership during Katrina. They say his response ruined his legacy. Do you agree or disagree? Argue your point with reasons and evidence.

SAY WHAT? Many citizens stepped up to help Katrina victims. Research other natural disasters. How have people helped? Describe ways in which people helped. Explain why people help others.

THINK ABOUT IT! New Orleans issued a mandatory evacuation for the first time during Hurricane Katrina. Why would people ignore an evacuation order? What would you do? Think about your resources and privileges. What allows you to evacuate or not?

Learn More

Brown, Don. *Drowned City: Hurricane Katrina and New Orleans.* New York, NY: Houghton Mifflin Harcourt, 2015.

Drimmer, Stephanie. *Ultimate Weatherpedia: The Most Complete Weather Reference Ever.* Washington, D.C.: National Geographic Kids, 2019.

Lowe, Alexander. *Natural Disasters in Infographics.* Ann Arbor, MI: Cherry Lake Publishing, 2021.

Orr, Tamra B. *Hurricane Katrina and America's Response.* Ann Arbor, MI: Cherry Lake Publishing, 2018.

Reina, Mary. *The Science of a Hurricane.* Ann Arbor, MI: Cherry Lake Publishing, 2015.

INDEX

ABOUT THE AUTHOR

Dr. Virginia Loh-Hagan is an author, former K–8 teacher, curriculum designer, and university professor. She's currently the director of the Asian Pacific Islander Desi American (APIDA) Center at San Diego State University. New Orleans is one of her favorite U.S. cities. She lives in San Diego with her one very tall husband and two very naughty dogs.